Sisterfriends

Words of Encouragement and Empowerment, From One Sister to Another

Linda Willis

Copyright © by Linda Willis, 1999

All Rights Reserved

Without limiting the rights under the copyright reserved above, no part of this publication may be reproduced, stored in, or introduced into a retrieval system, or transmitted in any form or by any means (electronic, mechanical, photocopying, recording, or otherwise) without prior written permission.

Bible verses were taken from the following translations:
KJV: The Holy Bible, King James Version

For permission requests and reorders, please contact:
Pastor Linda Willis
New Life of Memphis
6825 E. Holmes Rd.
Memphis, Tennessee 38141
Email: pastor@newlifeofmemphis.org
Phone: 901-370-6326

First printing 1999
Second printing 2003
Third printing 2018
ISBN# 978-1-7323035-0-8

Printed in the United States of America

Dedication

I wish to dedicate this book to my wonderful husband, Kevin B. Willis, Sr., to my children, Kelli and Kevin, Jr. and all of my *Sisterfriends* who are always there to cheer me on!

Foreword

Sisterfriends is a book filled with messages from the heart of God. Linda Willis is a dynamic preacher and an excellent and highly qualified author. Her experience as a pastor and counselor has given her great insight and knowledge, which she has effectively incorporated into her writings.

As her husband, I am honored to share the Angel of my life with readers everywhere. The brilliance of her spiritual genius and the passion in which she ministers will have a transforming and life changing effect on your life.

Bishop Kevin B. Willis, Sr.

Table of Contents

To My Sisterfriends…	9
Vision	11
Self-Esteem	13
Faith	15
Too Hard?	17
Free	18
One Step	20
Unmask	21
Confront	22
The Right Thing	23
Motherhood	25
Rain	26
A Cold Snap	27
Fear	29
Fractions	30
Love	31
Precious Moments	32
Truth	33
A Distorted Design	34
Sleepless Nights	36
God's Will	37
Loneliness	38
Clouds	40
Happy Birthday	41
Pregnant	44
Christmas	45
Achieving Success	46
Change	47
Red Flags	49
Woman Thou Art Loosed, Now What?	51
Standby	54

Control	56
Scars	58
Process	59
Too Soon	61
Fire	62
Desperate	63
Choose	64
Good Samaritan	65
Daddy	67
Heart	69
Lord	71
We Are Still Here!	73
Moments of Meditation	74
Prayer Petition	75
25 Ways to be Good to Yourself	76

Sisterfriends

Sisterfriends

To My Sisterfriends...

As women, we have so many experiences in common. Many of us have experienced the excitement of a new relationship, the thrill of becoming a wife, the joys of motherhood, the fulfillment of completing our education and the excitement of success. But we also share the pain of losing a relationship, the agony of loneliness, the shame of past mistakes, the fear of future failure, and the disappointment of lost dreams. Many of us board the rollercoaster or should I say treadmill of fixing, controlling, stuffing and binging to solve our problems.

Someone once said that the definition of *insanity* is trying the exact same thing over and over expecting to get a different result. I can definitely speak for myself and say that I was on my way to insanity. When my life was in turmoil, I continued to try the same methods for solving my problems that had not worked, expecting them to work the next time. I eventually resorted to just hiding my problems and acting as if everything was okay. And unfortunately, like some of you, the deep dark abyss of depression became my home.

But I praise God who looks beyond our faults and sees our needs! He sent virtuous women across my path who became a refuge for my weak soul. They gave me what only another *Sisterfriend* could give, sisterly love.

From there God planted a seed in my heart for other *Sisterfriends.* My compassion and concern causes me to want to share with women from all walks of life. You see, I survived my crisis and came out strong and victorious. But I can't really be free knowing that I have left others behind. My compassion and concern for other *Sisterfriends* caused me to want to give what I received! That opportunity came through my friend, the late Vivian Berryhill.

Sisterfriends is a compilation of words of encouragement and empowerment that I shared in a column for women, as a writer for the North Mississippi Herald, of which Vivian was the owner. She asked me would I put pen to paper and speak words of hope and inspiration to her female readers.

I later recognized that there was a broader audience that I needed to reach. And that audience includes you. I'm so excited about the opportunity to be a voice of encouragement and empowerment in your life. I believe that within the lessons learned through my challenges and struggles, there are definite blessings awaiting you!

From One Sister to Another,

Linda Willis

To My Sisterfriends...

As women, we have so many experiences in common. Many of us have experienced the excitement of a new relationship, the thrill of becoming a wife, the joys of motherhood, the fulfillment of completing our education and the excitement of success. But we also share the pain of losing a relationship, the agony of loneliness, the shame of past mistakes, the fear of future failure, and the disappointment of lost dreams. Many of us board the rollercoaster or should I say treadmill of fixing, controlling, stuffing and binging to solve our problems.

Someone once said that the definition of *insanity* is trying the exact same thing over and over expecting to get a different result. I can definitely speak for myself and say that I was on my way to insanity. When my life was in turmoil, I continued to try the same methods for solving my problems that had not worked, expecting them to work the next time. I eventually resorted to just hiding my problems and acting as if everything was okay. And unfortunately, like some of you, the deep dark abyss of depression became my home.

But I praise God who looks beyond our faults and sees our needs! He sent virtuous women across my path who became a refuge for my weak soul. They gave me what only another *Sisterfriend* could give, sisterly love.

From there God planted a seed in my heart for other *Sisterfriends.* My compassion and concern causes me to want to share with women from all walks of life. You see, I survived my crisis and came out strong and victorious. But I can't really be free knowing that I have left others behind. My compassion and concern for other *Sisterfriends* caused me to want to give what I received! That opportunity came through my friend, the late Vivian Berryhill.

Sisterfriends is a compilation of words of encouragement and empowerment that I shared in a column for women, as a writer for the North Mississippi Herald, of which Vivian was the owner. She asked me would I put pen to paper and speak words of hope and inspiration to her female readers.

I later recognized that there was a broader audience that I needed to reach. And that audience includes you. I'm so excited about the opportunity to be a voice of encouragement and empowerment in your life. I believe that within the lessons learned through my challenges and struggles, there are definite blessings awaiting you!

From One Sister to Another,

Linda Willis

Vision

Without a vision, the people perish (Proverbs 29:18). This scripture is not just relative to congregations of people, but to individuals as well. It is so easy to find yourself without a *vision*. I found myself at this point in my life several years ago. I was very busy being a wife and a mother, making sure that everyone had what they needed. When it came to thoughts of the future, my thoughts were always about *what my children were going to become*, and *where God was going to take my husband in his ministry*.

I am not exactly sure when I noticed this, but I began feeling that something was wrong. And as I am accustomed to doing, I began soul-searching. I found that I had become so consumed with everyone else's life, that I did not have one of my own.

I am not suggesting that being a good wife and mother is not important, because it is. But when we neglect ourselves in the process, things become imbalanced. If you are not careful, you find yourself with feelings of resentment, frustration, and even low self-esteem. I know, because I did! I was perishing because I did not have a *vision.* I was existing day to day, without any expectations for my future. I was created with purpose, but I was not pursuing it.

Revelation concerning who I was to become had ceased. When you do not have *vision*, you wander aimlessly through life, only bumping into success. God wants us to live

intentionally, to pursue life in Him and all that it has to offer. He wants us to live victoriously, striving to conquer, not waiting to be ambushed.

Today, you may be where I was some years ago. You are coping with the feelings of frustration, resentment, low self-worth, and possibly bitterness. You may even be bound by depression.

Sisterfriends, it is time for you to look at the possibilities of your own life. Only you can change your situation, and now is a good time to make the change. It's time to embrace the great things God wants to do in and through you. God declares in Jeremiah 29:11, *For I know the thoughts that I think toward you, saith the Lord, thoughts of peace, and not evil, to give you an expected end.* Open your mind and heart to receive the revelation that God has a plan for you! Yes, you! Let His *vision* enlarge your *vision*!

Self-Esteem

Self-esteem is the value given to one's self as a result of personal assessment. It is the attitude you have towards yourself. Now before you pat yourself on the back for having high *self-esteem*, let's take a closer look.

Self-esteem is determined by how you see yourself before anything is added. It is how you feel about yourself without the hair weave, nail tips, and designer clothes. It is how you think of yourself without a title or a degree. *Self-esteem* is how you feel when your money is funny and your friends are few. It is the value given to the original you!

I don't believe you can have a healthy relationship with others, until you have a healthy relationship with yourself. And it is impossible to have a healthy relationship with yourself, if you don't like you. When you don't like your breast because they are too small, or too large; the color of your skin is too light, or too dark; your hair too thin or your legs too small, you become your own worst enemy. Loving yourself requires that you love you…just as you are!

The reality is, there are also those whose *self-esteem* wavers, not because of their looks but because of their experiences. As little girls, some of you were emotionally abused, molested, or raped. You have been left with inner scars that make you feel unworthy and ashamed. As teenagers, some of you were down right disobedient and did things that you now regret. Maybe you had a baby out of wedlock; had so many sexual partners that you are too ashamed to count them; or did drugs and everything else that was out there to do. If your list is long or short, it is okay. What matters is who you are, not what you have done. Colossians 3:12 lets us know, that *We have been chosen of God, Holy and beloved.*

How do you build *self-esteem*? You've got to stop putting yourself down! I suggest that you sit down in front of the mirror and begin a new relationship with you. Re-introduce yourself to who you are on the inside. Remind yourself of how special you are. Rejoice over your successes and laugh at your mistakes. Forgive yourself for time wasted and forget about the opportunities missed. Appreciate your body, it's the only one you have. Believe in yourself and become your greatest supporter. Most of all, thank God for His wisdom. He knew exactly what He was doing when He created you!

Faith

What have you decided about your situation? Have you determined that you can't win? Have you just accepted that it is more than you can handle? Chances are you have not been using your shield of *faith*. The Bible tells us that *the shield of faith blocks the fiery darts of the enemy* (Ephesians 6:16). The devil (our enemy) uses penetrating suggestions of fear and failure to fill our minds (the true battleground) with worry, anxiety, and ultimately defeat. *Sisterfriend*, defeat cannot come until it is allowed to be established in your mind. When you shield yourself with *faith* in an all-powerful God, no enemy can overtake you.

So, before you hammer the last nail into the coffin or before you file spiritual bankruptcy, flex your *faith* one more time. I am not talking about just hanging on, but I am suggesting that you pursue a total resurgence of spiritual energy. I am talking about a realization of who you are in Christ.

It has been said, *heat makes things rise.* Well if the pressure is on in your life, rise to the occasion! Stop repeating what everybody else is saying about your outcome and say what God says: *No weapon formed against you will prosper* (Isaiah 54:17). Start believing in your heart that God is not a man that He should lie. His word will not return to Him void, but will accomplish what He desires, and achieve the purpose for which it was sent. Realize *faith* without works is dead.

Take a radical stand for the outcome you desire. When it's your last shot, you've got to give it all you've got. You have to look for the unexpected, speak the improbable, and do the unthinkable in order to receive the impossible. What do you have to lose? Who do you have to impress? *Sisterfriend,* stand up in *faith*!

Too Hard?

Is anything too hard for God? This question had to be answered when I reached the end of my rope and all I could do was tie a knot and hold on. Please understand, I am a *make it happen* kind of girl, who finds fulfillment in being the *go to person*! But there came a time when I had no solutions, no answers, and no way to fix things.

There comes a time in all of our lives when we realize our limitations. We are forced to tie a knot in our rope and hold on! But our ability to tie a knot and hold on is found in our belief that nothing is *too hard* for God.

Sisterfriend, you may have tried everything and are mentally and physically drained. But before you give up, I want you to LOOK UP! I know things can get hard, but you have to remind yourself that nothing is *too hard* for God. Encourage yourself by knowing that God sees your situation. Motivate yourself by believing that faith without work is dead. Whether it is a relationship gone bad, children who have gone astray, plans not working out, or just life (which can be hard in and of itself) you are not experiencing a problem that God has not solved before. Our responsibility is to walk by faith. So go ahead and tie the knot of faith and hold on until God works it out!

Free

Sisterfriend, it is a tragedy for people to walk around in bondage behind invisible bars of guilt and shame. But the greater tragedy is for those who are unbound, unchained, and *free*, to continue to live behind those bars of guilt and shame. They are ignorant to the fact that the door is unlocked, the bars are open, and the chain has been broken! Jesus tells us, *you shall know the truth, and the truth shall make you free* (John 8:32). Someone recently asked me, *how do you know when you are free?* Well this is the way I answered this question:

I am a native of Dallas, Texas where African Americans celebrate a holiday fondly called **Juneteenth.** On January 1, 1863, Abraham Lincoln signed the Emancipation Proclamation that freed the slaves. But it wasn't until the 19th of June in 1865 that the Black slaves in Texas got the news. Thus, our Independence Day became June 19th. It may have taken them a while to get the message, but the news finally reached Texas and the slaves living there, discovered they were *free*.

Sisterfriend, you are *free*! Your Emancipation Proclamation was signed over 2,000 years ago by our Savior, Jesus Christ, in red blood on an old wooden cross. The truth is that Christ has redeemed you from the bondage of sin and shame. God accepts you as you are because you are covered... not just in Christ's blood, but in His righteousness! This truth must travel beyond your present circumstances and past mistakes. It must go beyond your incessant fears and self-doubt and reach your *spirit*. Freedom must first be established in the spirit to be experienced in our lives. When your *spirit* finally gets this news, you will begin walking in liberty knowing that you are *free*! *Whom the Son has set free is free indeed (John 8:36)!*

One Step

As I was reading a book from one of my favorite authors, I read something that I thought was most powerful. The author said, *no matter how many steps are between you and God, He will make all but one.*

Sisterfriend, I can't think of a greater truth that needs to be embraced. This one truth gave me a greater understanding of how much God really loves me and the lengths He will take to pursue a closer relationship with me. It said to me that His desire is that there would be no distance between us. It suggested to me that there is an opportunity to be so close to Him, that I can hear Him when He whispers.

Herein lies the deeper truth. If you and I could hear Him clearly, we would understand the purpose for our lives and fulfill our destiny. If we could somehow hear Him when He calls, we could stay focused and not make so many mistakes. If we could just be near Him to hear when He whispers, we would receive the promises of victory and life everlasting.

Sisterfriend, there is a *step* that we must make. God will make 99, but we must put forth the effort to make that one. I urge you to begin assessing the *steps* that need to be taken to make your life better. You will find that there is *one step* that would make all of your other *steps* successful. That is the *step* toward Him!

Unmask

There is a movement in our society today toward comfort and ease. This has caused a great temptation in Christians to believe that the abundant life means a life without trouble. We now frown upon those who find themselves experiencing trials as if they are not true Christians. Something must be wrong with their relationship with God. Everybody has to come to Sunday service wearing their *every-thing-is-perfect-in-my-life* mask.

Sisterfriend, it is time for us to *unmask*! It is time for us to stop being embarrassed and ashamed. I am not suggesting that you go out and tell everybody your business, nor am I saying that you must wear sorrow on your face. I am speaking of liberation from the opinions of others. Opinions that cause us to go into hiding or to live in denial.

Sisterfriend, there is nothing new under the sun. Whatever problem you are having, somebody else has had it too. It does not necessarily mean you aren't living right, it could be that your number has come up on the enemy's hit list. But as the saying goes, *the devil meant it for evil, but God meant if for good.* So, go ahead, turn that trial into a testimony. Turn your shame into a sacrifice of praise, and your embarrassment into edification for someone else. You will be amazed at how many people you will bless!

Confront

Sisterfriend, the first step to taking off your *everything-is-perfect-in-my-life* mask is to *confront* the situation at hand. You must come out of hiding, and stop living in denial. You must make a decision to walk through the problem. No one enjoys experiencing pain or hardship, but if you are going to come out, you must go through. Closing yourself up in the house will not make it go away, neither does burying yourself in your work, make it disappear.

The Apostle Paul says that we must endure hardship as a good soldier. When the orders are given, whether in the cold of winter, or in the heat of summer, soldiers must go. It is the same with us! God orders our steps, and we must go through. Have you ever wondered, *Why now, Lord? Just when it looked as if everything was going well.* Have you ever said, *Lord, give me anything but this?* But the truth is, if God left it up to us, we would never experience trouble! So, in His omniscience, He chooses our path and schedules our struggles. *Sisterfriend,* I hope it will encourage you to know that He also decides the appointed time of our deliverance.

The Right Thing

Another area we should consider when we are facing difficult situations in our lives is how we treat those involved. I am no stranger to difficult situations or people. Just like anybody else, I have wanted to pay someone back for mistreating me. No matter how holy we profess to be, we all have the instinct to attack when we feel violated. However, we are more than instinctive beings. We have been created with a consciousness (an awareness) of right and wrong. God wants us to use this awareness as a means to choose to do the *right thing*. Two wrongs have never made anything right. I believe I have made some bad situations worse by reacting wrongly to them.

Sisterfriend, doing the *right thing* begins with pure motives. This has to do with what is in our heart. We have to get rid of the desire to prove a point or get revenge. These desires, when carried out, lower us to the level of the other person. The only thing that has been proven when we lower ourselves to the malicious level of another, is the power they have over us.

What can you do instead, when dealing with a difficult person? Jesus says, *love your enemies, do good to those who hate you, bless those who curse you, pray for those who mistreat you. Do to others as you would have them to do to you.*

Sisterfriend, this really works! Love has a way of disarming the most difficult person, and prayer does change things.

Sisterfriends

Our purpose for doing the *right thing* is not just to disarm difficult people, but to please God in all that we do. I hold fast to the thought that when our ways please God, He will make even our enemies to be at peace with us. We will not only be at peace with our enemies, but we will be able to sleep at night because we will be at peace with ourselves.

Motherhood

Motherhood is an awesome responsibility with only one chance to get it right. There are no rehearsals or retakes. You do the best you can do, with the knowledge that you have, and pray that you are doing something right. Even with doing it right, there are no guarantees. It is by the grace of God that our children succeed.

Sisterfriend, I think that it is a pity that mothers are celebrated only one day out of the year. Secretaries get a whole week; African American History gets a month. Think about it ... there would be no secretaries to appreciate without mothers and no African American history to celebrate, if it wasn't for the strength and determination of mothers.

Well, from one mother to another, I salute you! Because I know the challenges you face and the love that you demonstrate as a caregiver, I appreciate you! As the hand that rocks the cradle you possess power, and as matriarchs of society you exude wisdom. I honor you today, and every day!

Rain

Do you remember the saying, *April showers bring May flowers?* It reminds us that not only does a plant need sunshine to make it grow, it also needs *rain*. Although *rain* is an inconvenience to us, it is God's way of providing a necessary nutrient to the earth.

Even in our lives, *Sisterfriend,* we need some *rain* to help us grow. Our lives would dry up and die from complacency and stagnation if every day was sunny. The storms of life we go through serve as showers of experience that give us the wisdom and determination. Each trial presents an opportunity for us to grow in character and strength.

Rain not only waters the earth, but it also cleanses it. Likewise, those tears we shed act as a cleansing agent to rid our soul of emotional pollutants such as, anger, hatred, anxiety, and frustration. Crying allows us to become vulnerable to the elements of life called pain and sorrow. Tears wash away our pride and self-will. All of us could use this kind of cleansing!

Sisterfriend, if you are experiencing a rainy season in your life, if it seems as if a torrential downpour is flooding your existence, know that growth is on the way. The *rain* has not come to drown you, but to water the seeds of your life so that you will grow.

A Cold Snap

Not long ago, we experienced an unexpected change in weather that threw us all for a loop. This *cold snap* as my mother would call it, came after the flowers began to bloom, trees began to bud, and we began to shed our winter clothes. Just when we thought the winter was over, we found ourselves experiencing unexpected freezing temperatures and snow flurries. The only consolation I could find was in knowing that this was a temporary condition; spring would definitely come.

Sisterfriend, like the trees, you may have started to bud. You started making steps towards improving your life. Maybe you were coming out of debt, had lost seven of those 20 pounds, or had packed Mr. No-Good's clothes. Some of you finally cleaned out your emotional closets and began working toward your dreams. You thought you had made it through winter. And just when you got the courage to spring forth, a *cold snap* occurred.

A *cold snap* in life is anything that takes you two steps backwards just after you've made one step forward. Sometimes it is a door closed in your face, a lack of support from loved ones, or you simply fell off the wagon.

Life is like nature; it goes in cycles. In the midst of whatever has caused your setback, you must believe that it's temporary. Remember, we do not throw away our summer clothing when winter comes, we only pack them away. So don't throw away your goals and dreams. You may have to pack them away for a moment, but they are too valuable to discard.

Never make permanent decisions based on temporary circumstances. If you are experiencing a *cold snap* in your life, hang on, Spring is coming!

Fear

As you know, gusty winds are typical for the month of March. The other day, I came out of the hair salon with my hair freshly done and intact, but before I could get to the car, the wind had blown it all out of place. While driving, I even found myself clutching the steering wheel trying to keep my car steady as the violent winds blew. This brought to mind a sermon my husband preached concerning *fear*.

He said that the spirit of *fear* is like the wind. It is a powerful force that you cannot see. When it blows in our lives, it wreaks havoc.

Sisterfriend, fear has the power to throw things in your life out of place. Your confidence, self-esteem, and determination can be tossed around as the leaves are blown from one yard to another. Things that you know you can do and goals that you can achieve, can become torn and tattered by a sudden gust of *fear*. Like the wind kicks up dust, and impairs your ability to see, *fear* also kicks up anxiety and doubt that hinders your ability to believe. If you don't hold on tightly to what is in your heart, you will find yourself blown off course.

Sisterfriend, when you experience the violent wind of *fear* tossing you to and fro, when the dust of anxiety and doubt is flying and you cannot see your way clearly; cling to the Word of God, and let faith be your guide. Realize that like in the month of March, the wind of *fear* is typical of this time in your life…it will pass.

Fractions

As I talk with women who are single, I find some view themselves as *fractions*. *Fractions* are *Sisterfriends* who feel incomplete without a man, and spend most of their time looking for him. They believe that whatever is lacking in their lives will be found in a relationship. Some *Sisterfriends* will not take a vacation, enjoy a sunset, or even a dinner if not accompanied by a man.

Now I am not criticizing any woman for *wanting* a man. Desiring companionship is a part of being human. Even God said, it is not good for man to be *alone*! Oftentimes, we are under the notion that having companionship is somehow going to make us complete. We believe that having *Mr. Right* will make everything right in our lives. So we put everything on hold until he shows up.

Well, my *Sisterfriends*, if this describes you, it is time to take your life off of *pause*. If you are waiting for *Mr. Right* so that you can finally be complete, you have missed him! God is the only one who can do for you what you cannot do for yourself. He designed relationships to *compliment* us, not *complete* us. Colossians 2:10 says, "and you are complete in Him, who is the head of all principality and power." That's right! You are complete...a whole person...not a fraction! So go ahead and enjoy your whole life! And when he does come along, he will be icing on your already whole cake.

Love

Love is…

The end of this statement is being completed every day of our lives. It is shown in how we treat others as well as how we treat ourselves. Through the *love*, God gives us the unique opportunity to express what is divine on a human level. I cannot think of anything more heavenly than the relationship between a man and a woman. Words cannot describe it when it is right, because it is not made on earth. God does it!

Sisterfriend, what do you think *love* is? I believe *love* is whatever someone needs that you can give. *Love* is the least expensive present you can give and the most valuable gift you can receive. It can be a warm smile, words of encouragement, some understanding, a little personal space, or a whole lot of affection.

When given, *love* is the most powerful, life-changing gift one can experience. I know because my life was changed thirty-one years ago when God gave me *love* wrapped up in Kevin Willis, my husband. Kevin's *love* has been whatever I needed, that he had. It has given life to two beautiful children, produced strength to overcome life's struggles, patience to handle our differences, and kindness to make it all worthwhile.

Precious Moments

A few years ago during Black History Month, I had my daughter to check out library books on African American women. One day as we chatted, she shared with me her feelings about the stories she had read. She was troubled by the injustices that were endured by the women she read about. I took this opportunity to help her understand that she had come from a rich heritage of women. Women who withstood the tremendous struggles of racism to give her freedom. I explained how those women fought overwhelming battles of sexism to give her opportunity to make her own choices. It was because of those women; she could now excel as far as her mind will take her. I further admonished that she had an obligation to take advantage of the privileges now available to her so that their labor would not be in vain.

Suddenly, I remembered being a little girl, hearing my mother say the same things to me. I could hear the words emanating from my own mother's voice: *You can be anything you want to be. The way has already been paved.* Those words inspired me more than any textbook. They have lived with me to this very day.

Sisterfriend, what an opportunity God gives us as mothers. He allows us to empower the next generation for excellence. I hope you will use those *precious moments* with your *Little Sisterfriends,* to share the powerful legacy of their ancestry. This is your opportunity to speak into their lives, and inspire them to achieve greatness.

Truth

Whenever I am facing a difficult situation, the first thing I ask God is that He would open my eyes that I may see the *truth*. I want to be able to distinguish between what is right and wrong, and what is permanent and what is temporary. These distinctions may seem simple, but when facing complex situations, our judgement can be clouded. Right begins to look wrong and wrong starts looking right. It is easy to find ourselves mixing *truth* with feelings, and facts with opinions.

Sisterfriend, I can honestly say that I have gotten off the pathway of *truth*, and traveled down the road of false assumptions a time or two! I assumed a delay was a denial and a closed door was a locked door. I have foolishly allowed myself to become depressed and filled with anxiety over things that were only temporary.

Feelings of hopelessness will overwhelm you if you do not keep your eyes focused on *truth*. In reality, *truth* is not founded upon feelings, nor is it based upon opinions! And what about opinions? Everyone can tell you what they would do if they were you, but the *truth* is, they are not. You have to seek an understanding of your situation from God. He proclaims that He is *truth*. Everything in your life must be measured according to His word. *Sisterfriend,* when you walk in *truth* it stabilizes your mind, and allows you to make sound decisions. It enhances your ability to receive direction from God; therefore, creating an atmosphere for your deliverance.

A Distorted Design

A well-known magazine published an article that grappled with a God who could allow women to endure the atrocities of sexual abuse by predators, relatives, and even their own fathers. I wanted to speak to this issue in hopes of bringing some help and healing to some *Sisterfriend* who is struggling with this same question.

Women throughout history have been victimized by those who through the vehicle of sex, have stolen their purity, possessions, and peace of mind. Consequently, many women have a marred view of sexuality based on their painful experiences. It is often difficult to understand where God is in all of this. But we must make the distinction between God and His creation. It was mankind that distorted what God purposed to be *good.* This should not come as a surprise because mankind has had a proclivity to destroy everything God made, including one another, since the days of Adam and Eve. This abuse of something that God intended to be beautiful has left women feeling guilty, ashamed, isolated, and worthless.

But to really know the real purpose of something, we must go back to its original design. God not only designed sex to allow us to become co-creators with Him in the producing of offspring, but He designed the physical coming together of man and woman to provide mutual gratification, and express the highest level of intimacy between two people.

Has this design been distorted? Yes, but remember, the Bible says *you shall know the truth and the truth shall make you free* (John 8:32). I want some *Sisterfriend* today, to be made free knowing the truth.

Sisterfriend, you are free to disconnect the meaning of intimacy from the painful experience of sexual abuse. You are free to put blame in its rightful place. You are free to appreciate the characteristics of your femininity. You are free to own your own desires and passions and free to know the feeling of oneness through physical intimacy. *Sisterfriend*, you are free!

Sleepless Nights

In our efforts to fix our lives and the people in them, we often find ourselves experiencing *sleepless nights*. We focus on what is not right and what is not working out, leaving little room for noticing what is. Being blessed is not just a matter of getting what we want, but also appreciating what we have. Life, health, and a sound mind are blessings that get overlooked because of the despair over our desires. However, without these blessings all others would be useless. *Sisterfriend,* I encourage you to take a moment to breathe, relax, and focus on the good, instead of the bad. Chances are you will end your nights counting blessings instead of sheep.

God's Will

Have you ever found yourself truly seeking *God's will* for your life? I have. You know how it is when you really want to do the right thing.

While reading my Bible one day, I discovered a scripture that says, *In everything give thanks, for this is the will of God in Christ Jesus concerning you* (1 Thessalonians 5:18). *God's will* for my life was right there, spelled out in black and white. *Give thanks.* How simple, yet profound. *God's will* for my life is a position, not a purpose.

He is concerned about my attitude; not my altitude. He desires that I have an attitude of gratitude toward Him. In every situation, I am to give thanks. Most of us do not have a problem with being thankful for the good experiences, but what about the bad? This is our true challenge in accepting *God's will* for us to give thanks in everything.

What is there to be thankful about in tragedy, hurt, and pain? *Sisterfriend,* it is *God's will* that we look deeper into those not-so-good experiences, and see Him. Our thankfulness comes in knowing that He is there. Even when we do not know it. He is there.

Whether we allow His presence to comfort us during these times, is our choice, but He is there. Thanksgiving should be every day, for this is the will of God in Christ Jesus concerning you.

Loneliness

As I sat down to write today, I began to think about those who are experiencing *loneliness*. While many people are anxiously awaiting the end of the day, others face it with dread. Some of you will have an empty seat at the dinner table tonight. Others will find it hard to live up to the expectations of others. I realize it is difficult to act happy when you are hurting inside. I am not talking about physical pain … I am speaking of the emotional agony of *loneliness* and grief.

I recently shared this with a lady whose husband passed away. She questioned whether she was abnormal because she was still grieving his death. I replied, *I don't believe that anyone can decide what is the proper amount of time to grieve over someone with whom you spent 43 years of your life with.*

I do know that God sent His Son to heal the broken-hearted and if you will submit yourself to Him, He will soothe your sorrows. I also understand that some of you will be lonely because you don't have that *special someone* in your life. Maybe it is due to a relationship that did not work out or you lost your love to death.

So much advice is given on how to handle this difficult time. Some will tell you to keep yourself busy, others advise to share your feelings with a friend. I'm not going to tell you what I think you should do, instead, I would like to tell you what I am going to do.

I am going to lift you up before God daily, in my prayers. I don't know who you are, but God knows. I am not just telling you this because it sounds good to say. I am saying this because you are my *Sisterfriend,* and I care. I cannot cure your *loneliness*, neither can I heal your pain, but I can pray to the One who can. I believe the power of God can help you overcome every challenge that you face. So, in the upcoming days, when nights become long, and the days are difficult, if you begin to feel like you just cannot make it, remember you've got a *Sisterfriend* who is praying for you!

Clouds

On a recent trip, I glanced out of the window of the airplane and saw *clouds* that looked like glimpses of heaven. When we landed, I got into the car, looked into the sky and saw storm *clouds*. As I reflected on this experience, I thought about how many times I had judged life based on where I was sitting. In the plane, the *clouds* looked different because I was riding above them.

Sisterfriends, just like in the airplane, we have the ability to *ride* above the *clouds*! We can see problems as challenges, dead ends as turning points, and difficult people as opportunities to give love. Make a decision today about the *clouds* in your life. They can either be your sign of a future storm or your vision of a glorious future.

Happy Birthday!

Recently I celebrated my *birthday*. The celebration was not one with balloons, food and friends. It was more of a mental party with all my experiences as guest. For the first time, I could handle seeing them all together! The good experiences, the bad, and the ones that hurt, had all come to celebrate this year of growth with me. This was really special for them because they all finally felt welcomed!

You see, I used to only want to remember the good times. The bad were too embarrassing and the ones that hurt were too painful!

As we began to reminisce, I could appreciate them all. The good experiences had given me the much-needed spurts of joy and happiness that I needed to maintain self-worth and feel loved. The bad experiences had developed in me patience, determination, and courage. The ones that hurt had produced strength, compassion, and most of all the ability to forgive. I could see that they had made me the person I am today!

Another person attended my celebration, the most important guest of all. It was the Holy Spirit! His voice could be heard above all the rest. He said: *My child, none of these experiences could have happened had I not allowed them. I opened the door of your life and decided what would come in. They have all been working together for your good. Through them, I have been able to give you your most valuable asset, wisdom! I have given you a discerning heart to travel beneath the surface to see truth. I have given you the ability to apply what you have learned so that you will exercise righteous judgement.*

Then He gave me future instructions from His word in Proverbs 4:6:

Do not forsake wisdom, and she will protect you; love her, and she will watch over you. Wisdom is supreme therefore get wisdom. Though it cost all you have, get understanding. Esteem her, and she will exalt you; embrace her, and she will honor you. She will set a garland of grace on your head, and present you with a crown of splendor.

They all wished me *happy birthday* and left, except for one, the Holy Spirit! He is my constant companion. I will forever cherish this celebration; it was the most meaningful party I ever had.

Sisterfriend, today does not have to be your *birthday* for you to have this wonderful celebration. This celebration can take place whenever you are ready to embrace your whole life. We spend a lot of time running from our past, trying to escape our present and avoid our future. *Sisterfriend,* the ultimate truth is that until the day you die, your life will always consist of a past, present, and future!

The powerful revelation in this is that God designed it that way to bring His purpose forth in your life. These three phases are constantly rotating in your life to grow you in wisdom. Can you hear the Psalmist saying, *Lord teach us to number our days, that we may apply our hearts unto wisdom* (Psalm 90:12).

Every heartache you have felt, every tear that you have cried, every friend that stabbed you in the back, every man that did you wrong, every plan that did not work, and every moment of happiness that you have experienced, has had wisdom wrapped inside of it. Did you get it? If so, throw a party! Invite another *Sisterfriend* if you want, she needs to celebrate too. (Now that my mascara is running down my face, and I feel a dance in my feet, I better move on).

Pregnant

The story of the Virgin Mary and the immaculate conception has been told a million times. It recounts the moments in history when God chose a humble young woman to birth the Savior of the world. However, this story actually is about more than one woman. It speaks of every woman who is *pregnant* with potential. This story demonstrates the power of the Holy Spirit to indwell every woman and manifest a miracle. This divine pregnancy is the abilities, passions, and talents waiting to be delivered from the womb of every *Sisterfriend.*

Sisterfriend, like Mary, we face tremendous challenges. The uncertainty of how God will use us and the possibility of people in our lives not understanding will cause us to have to walk in faith. For comfort, the Holy Spirit will lead us to an Elizabeth who can relate and celebrate with us, because she is *pregnant* too.

Sisterfriend, something is living within all of us that when birthed could minister to humanity. There is a miracle waiting to come forth in you because you have been chosen, just like Mary. You are *highly favored, a*nd God is with you. Make her-story, your-story by believing that God can do the impossible in your life, *and that it will be done unto you according as He hath said it.*

Christmas

Christmas is the most challenging time of the year for many women. It is when mothers feel pressured to buy toys they really can't afford. Wives frantically search for the right gift for the in-laws without help from husbands. Lonely women feel the need to find a man or hold on to the one they meant to get rid of earlier in the year. The amazing part about all of this is that we will spend December 26th thanking God that it is over, and wake up January 1st anticipating doing it all over again.

Well I believe it is time to liberate ourselves from this seasonal bondage. Freedom does not come by accident; it has to be planned. My plan is to make *Christmas* an expression of what I have to give and not what someone else wants.

Sisterfriend, love and attention are the most valuable gifts we can give our children, and it doesn't cost anything. Other family and friends are given the gift of our time which never has to be returned because of the wrong color or size. *And a word to the wise...* having a man just to make it through the holidays is like having a temporary job. The benefits are minimal, and you know it is not going to last!

Sisterfriend, remember *Christmas* is not about how much money you spend, nor is it about swapping gifts with people who already have. It is not even about snuggling with someone on a cold winter's night. Jesus is the reason for the season. He is the greatest gift God gave. Use your freedom in Him to make this season an expression of His love.

Achieving Success

Have you taken the time to seek God's purpose for your life? If so, write down and post it where you can see it every day. *Write the vision, and make it plain upon tables, that he may run that readeth it* (Habakkuk 2:2). Having a vision, goal, or dream does not require that you know how it is going to be accomplished. Just take the time to get in touch with what's in your heart. Most of the time God's will is hidden in your heart. List your strengths, passions, and secret dreams. Talk to people who know you well and get their opinion of your capabilities. Be careful of who you choose to talk with. They should only be people who are positive and aggressive. A person who is struck in a rut is not going to be too inspiring. Choose friends who are willing to dream with you.

The next step is to establish objectives that are in alignment with your vision. Write them down too. Objectives are smaller goals that will contribute to your ultimate vision. Give yourself a time limit for accomplishing each objective. A time limit is important because it helps you overcome the demon of procrastination.

Now *Sisterfriend*, it's time to put your walking shoes on and hit the pavement. If you desire to go back to school, complete an application. If it is in your heart to start your own business, develop your business plan.

Proverbs 13:4 states: *The soul of the sluggard (lazy) desires and gets nothing, but the soul of the diligent (attentive) is made prosperous (successful).*

Change

There is a saying that says *If you do what you have always done, you are going to get what you've always gotten.* This means if you go in the same direction that you've always gone, you're going to end up at the same place you've always been. Now this may be okay for some, but most of us sincerely want more, better, or simply want for things to *change* in our lives.

Sisterfriend, if you really want to get something different, you've got to do something different. You've got to work the problem out a different way; you've got to go down a different road. Sometimes, you even have to get rid of the old. We got rid of scrub boards and clothes lines when we got washing machines and dryers. We put down our old typewriters when we discovered that we could use computers that not only would allow us to make correction, but would also save the document so that we wouldn't have to retype it. I am not suggesting that everything that is old must be replaced. There are some things that have lasting value. But those things that have diminished in their effectiveness, or are not producing the outcome we desire, must be abandoned for what will.

I am different from what I was ten years ago, even five years ago. My faith is more intense and my worship is much stronger. I replaced ways of solving my problems with prayer and living by the word of God. Why did I make these changes? Because, if I had not changed and embraced God's ability to do a new thing in my life, I would have been swallowed up by my problems or the difficulties of living would have choked me to death.

Sisterfriend, what changes do you need to make in order for your life to be better? Let the *change* begin!

Red Flags

I believe the Holy Spirit gives us signs to direct the path of our lives much like the signs that are used in traffic. The intent of signs is to give direction to the driver so that he or she may reach their desired destination quickly, and safely. The problem occurs, however, when we ignore such signs! When we are too impatient to wait or too proud to stop, the result is usually a major collision! If any of us were willing to be honest, we would admit that there have been times in our lives when we have traveled through life ignoring the *warning* signs. Some people call them hunches, intuition, your first mind, or feelings on the back of your neck. I simply call them *red flags.*

Sisterfriend, red flags are those signals that you get when something is wrong. And what I've noticed in us as women is *red flags* are most overlooked and ignored in relationships with men. *Red flags* are those times in which he has said to you with his behavior that he isn't ready for commitment. A *red flag* is when helping him begins to hurt you. Another *red flag* is when you have to lie to yourself to maintain your love for him. How many times have you said after a relationship is over, *I saw it coming, I knew it all along, I just didn't want to accept it?*

What causes us to run through the red lights of life? What makes us fail to slow down at the yield sign? What motivates us to keep going when the sign says detour? *Sisterfriend,* it is time to figure out *what* is behind the wheel of your life? Is your life being

Sisterfriends

driven by something other than you? Is it fear, loneliness or desperation? Maybe it is pride or lack of self-control? Are you in the driver's seat and not sure about what you are doing? The word of God tells us, *Trust in the Lord with all thine heart and lean not to your own understanding. Acknowledge Him in all thy ways, and He shall direct thy path (*Proverbs 3:5-6).

Sisterfriend, when the bells are ringing and the whistle is blowing and the *red flag* is slapping you in the face, it might just be the Holy Spirit speaking to you. If you listen, you could avoid a collision.

Woman Thou Art Loosed...
Now What?

How have you been spending your time since you were healed, delivered, and set free? I am the first to celebrate with you over the fact that you have been set free, but when you finish praising, what is your purpose?

Sisterfriend, we have a tendency to only focus on short term results. Our concentration is usually on deliverance from the immediate problem, the crisis, or the drama that is going on in our lives. But I suggest to you that there was a long-range goal that God had in mind when He delivered you. You may not have recognized it, but God brought you out to bring you up to a new level of commitment.

Like everyone else that Jesus healed, we must make a decision either to detach ourselves and go on our way or dedicate ourselves to Him. Did you forget about Him after He *loosed* you? Do you pray like you used to when Johnny would not come home at night, when we thought he had another woman, when he wouldn't bring his paycheck home? What are you doing now that you've been *loosed*? What is your relationship like with Jesus now that the cancer is gone?

Let me tell you the danger in choosing to detach and go home. You have a tendency to get caught and taken captive again by the devil. When we go back home we get comfortable and relaxed. We start operating out of a superficial sense of confidence *Thank You Lord for delivering me, but I think I can handle it from here!* That's how we end up in another bad relationship. That's how we end up getting fired form another job. That's how we end up making more bad decisions.

A *loosed* woman should have a deep sense of appreciation for her deliverance and devotion to her deliverer. Do you appreciate what God has done for you? Do you remember when you had to do your own hair because you could not afford to get it professionally done? How about when you alternated your dresses every other Sunday, because you didn't have but two? What about when you had to take your lunch to work, or when you and your husband only had one car to drive, or worse, you had to ride the bus. My level of devotion is increasing right now!

With devotion also comes a sense of duty. You understand that God used somebody to preach a sermon, say an encouraging word, or pray a prayer for you. You know that if God hadn't laid it on somebody's heart to call you when you were at your lowest, give you that book that changed your life, stick some money in your hand when you were broke, let you cry it out, you wouldn't be here today. Therefore, you commit to investing yourself in the lives of others.

Sisterfriend, there is purpose in your liberty. You have been *loosed* to do something that you could not do in the bondage that you were in. The hands that were tied, the feet that were shackled and the mind that was bound are now free! Now what?

Standby

A while ago, I had the opportunity of flying *standby* on one of the local airlines. I was flying *standby* because I had been given a free pass by a friend who worked for the airline. The drawback to the free pass is that you are given a seat only if there are any seats left after all the paid passengers have boarded. Therefore, you must "stand by" until you are lucky enough to get a flight that is not full, thus its name *standby*. Of course, *standby* is great because it's free and it works if you have a lot of free time and don't mind getting bumped. But if you are trying to get somewhere at a specific time, if you don't want to wait in line only to find out the flight is full, or if you don't want to have to go back home and wait until the next day to see if you can get a flight out, you had better pay for your ticket!

As I sat in the airport waiting to see if I would be able to get on my choice of flights, I thought about how many of us fly through life on *standby*. You see, all around me were people who had paid for their seat on the plane, so consequently they were assured a seat. But there I was with my fate left to chance and luck. And then, I had to also be lucky enough to beat other people in line who were flying *standby*, as I was.

I began to think about how many of us are depending on what happens in someone else's life to determine what happens in ours. Our choices hinge upon their choices and our decisions their decisions. Sadly, as in the case with the airline, we get bumped all too often. Our goals and dreams are, once again, put on the back burner. Maybe tomorrow, maybe next year, maybe the next flight.

Sisterfriend, how many flights have you been bumped off because you were flying *standby?* Well as for me, I made a conscious decision in my life not to travel *standby* anymore. I decided that I was going to pay for the right to make some choices about my destiny and not have to take what was left. I have paid in sacrifice, hard work, and commitment for the privilege of having a reserved seat in life. *Sisterfriend, you* have a purpose and destiny in life and only a certain amount of time to get there. You can't ride through life on a free pass expecting to get anywhere fast. You have to be willing to pay your way to some places with sacrifice and hard work

Now, I know my super-spiritual *Sisterfriends* are saying, *my faith will get me there.* And this is partly true. But now look in the mirror and tell yourself, *faith without works is dead. Sisterfriend,* make sure you have a reserved seat!

Control

Sharing with many of my friends, I have noticed a common theme among us. We all want *control*! Whether it is *control* over our finances, relationships, job situations, weight or feelings, we are desperately trying to get a handle on something. On the surface, it may appear that we are just strong-willed women with a need to have things done our way. But as I scratch beneath the surface, I find that most of our desire to *control* is driven by fear. Our controlling personalities have been formed out of experiences that left us feeling vulnerable and unsettled. We have gone through experiences that felt like a roller coaster ride and all we could do is hang on for dear life. When getting off the ride, with our stomach turned upside down and our head spinning, we vowed to never get on that ride again!

Sisterfriend, fear is a powerful force that can take *control* of you. You find yourself in overdrive, holding on too tight, and unable to let go. Do you find yourself obsessed with having things, *just right?* Do you have a vision of a *perfect* relationship? Do you tend to get tense when things are off schedule? Do you insist on knowing every detail of a plan? You may just have a *control* problem. You may be out of *control*. The truth is that there are things we cannot *control*, like other people and what they do (just to name a few).

One day, I sat down and made a list of what I could control. I must tell you that my list was rather short. I realized that basically I could only *control* me, my opinion, beliefs, decisions, and actions. Suddenly, I remembered the *Serenity Prayer* and knew this was exactly what I needed to pray:

Lord, grant me the serenity to
Accept the things the I cannot change,
The courage to change the things I can,
And the wisdom to know the difference.

From one recovering *control* addict to another, here are a few tips:
1. Nobody is perfect, including you.
2. Even though we want the *best, good* is not so bad.
3. Happiness come from what happens-in-us.
4. Life is a journey, not a destination, and it must be traveled one day at a time.

Scars

Scars are unsightly blemishes left behind from damage done to us. Usually we try to hide or cover them, or at least not talk about them. We not only have outer *scars*, but we have inner ones, those not visible to the human. Unfortunately, we deal with these the same way. But I would like for you to take another look at your *scars*. You see, *scars* are not an indication that you are wounded, but that you are healed! Now maybe you didn't heal the way you wanted to, without the wound leaving a trace. Most wounds do. But you did heal. Your scar is actually a testimony of the depth and degree of trauma that you experienced and the magnitude of your deliverance. It says where you've been and how far you've come. Don't hide it. It is a medal of honor that says you have been in battle and you survived.

Process

I've discovered something this year that really caused me to grow to another spiritual level. It was as if somebody turned the light on in my dark room of frustration. My phenomenal discovery was that *not only does God have a purpose for my life, but He also has a process, and the process is just as important as the purpose.* Wow! Man! Whew! What a revelation! If I had known this ten years ago, I would have calmed down and enjoyed the ride much better.

You see, what caused a lot of my frustration and anxiety with the adversity that would arise in my life was that I thought it was deterring, or preventing me from reaching my purpose. However, what I found out on a much deeper level is, (that you may not be ready to receive yet, but I'll give it to you anyway)...*the process is a big part of the purpose!*

I am convinced that if God were only concerned about *the end,* He would move much faster in our deliverance. I now believe that the *process* is His real agenda. Think about it... God could allow any of us, in an instant, to reach our goals and attain our purpose, but instead he takes us through the *process* of experiencing mountains and valleys, deserts and rivers, starting and stopping, waiting and wandering (and the list goes on). However, when you really look at it, it is the *process* that develops our relationship with Him. The *process* activates our faith. The *process* builds our strength.

The *process* strengthens our character. God becomes the artist chiseling out the masterpiece. Each cut shapes us into what He wants us to be. Every area of resistance requires more time and pressure. Each smooth place is further refined and polished. If you have a relationship with God and have been through anything, I am sure you can see some virtue, some ability, or some wisdom that has been developed that you didn't have before.

Now, what do you do with revelation? Calm down, take a deep breath, release the anxiety, exercise patience, and embrace what you are going through as being a part of the *process.* You'll be glad you did!

Too Soon

My husband and I were in a hurry trying to make it to an appointment and found ourselves in the thick of traffic. Feeling the anxiety of possibly being late for the appointment, we began to discuss what we should do. My opinion was that we should take the next exit and find an alternate route. He, on the other hand, felt that we were giving up *too soon*, and should wait it out, (since traffic was moving, although at a slow pace). Well, I reluctantly agreed and to my surprise, we were able to make it through. However, as I glanced over at the exit that we would have taken, I saw a complete traffic jam. There had been an accident on the off ramp and traffic was at a standstill. Of course, bells began to go off in my head about the life application of this experience.

How often it is that we become anxious and impatient because we are not getting something or somewhere fast enough. It becomes so tempting to deviate from the route only to find out that we got off *too soon*. If only we could have practiced patience and seen it through.

Sisterfriend, things may be moving a little slow for you right now but stay your course, sooner and sometimes later you are assured to get there.

There's a way that seemeth right unto man, but the end thereof is destruction (Philippians 3:19).

Fire

We must know the difference between the fiery darts of the enemy and the cleansing *fire* of the Holy Spirit. James 1:13 says *Let no one say when he is tempted, 'I am tempted by God'; for God cannot be tempted by evil nor does He Himself tempt anyone.* There are some fires we go through that are self-inflicted. We are responsible for igniting them and must suffer the consequences!

But there is a *fire* that is ordained by God for our benefit. It has not happened to destroy us, but to destroy the things in our lives that are not like Him. When we are able to recognize who is at work, we can know better how to respond. I am not suggesting that this is an easy task, or one that will always be accomplished at the onset of our troubles. Life is so complex; it does not always present a simple equation. Events happen so quickly and often do not afford us an opportunity to put every situation under the microscope for analysis.

Sisterfriend, do not spend your time avoiding this *fire*, nor delaying it, but seek God for His divine strength to go through. Avoiding the opportunity to allow God to burn away the impurities keep Him from exposing the gold that it is covering. A delayed *fire* is a delayed blessing!

Desperate

In the news, a couple of years ago, was the account of a man, who got in his car along with his little children, drove to a bank in the middle of the day and robbed it. Everyone talked about how stupid he was, for it appeared that his plan was not well thought out. He also seemed very cold and callous to have taken his children along with him. However, the only thing I could think about was how *desperate* he must have been to do what he did, when and how he did it! Now we could all argue that he had other options, but evidently, he couldn't see them at the time.

Desperation occurs when we can't see options. *Desperation* will cause you to do what you said you would never do. It will cause you to throw off the restraints in attempt to solve your problem. When you are walking through a dilemma and feel like the next step could lead to your demise, if not careful, you will behave irrationally and irresponsibly to save yourself.

Sisterfriend, no matter how hard it may seem, no matter how difficult the circumstances, no matter how extreme the trial, you must not give in to *desperation.* God has the solution, but you must trust Him enough to wait. He will deliver you. *God is your refuge and your strength, a very present help in the time of trouble* (Psalm 46:1). Seeking refuge any other way will only get you into more trouble.

Choose

Some of us have fooled ourselves into believing that life hangs in a state of suspension as long as we don't make decisions. We believe that we are buying time when we don't give a definite answer.

Sisterfriend, not *choosing* is *choosing*. You have chosen by default. This means that you *choose* to accept whatever happens. Not making decisions about your life is like not voting on Election Day. You get stuck with what someone else decides. What are you stuck with? How long will you allow others to decide for you?

This is not about whether or not you should leave your husband or your job. This is about you becoming proactive in your own life. God even honors your right to *choose*. He says, *I have set before you, life and death, blessing and cursing; therefore, choose life, that both you and your descendants may live* (Deuteronomy 30:15).

The Good Samaritan

A man was going down from Jerusalem to Jericho, when he fell into the hands of robbers. They stripped him of his clothes, beat him and went away leaving him half dead. I believe the image of this wounded man can be enlarged to represent those in our society who have been stripped of resources and opportunities and left to die in mediocrity. He represents those who started out with the same intentions and passions that you and I did, but are now stripped, robbed, and left half dead. Life is filled with robbers and circumstances that distract and deter the best of intentions. These circumstances can steal desire and ultimately demolish a future.

What's interesting about this story is three men are given an opportunity to help this man. All three have a chance to repair what had been damaged, but the only one that stopped to help was the *Samaritan*. History tells us that *Samaritans* were looked down upon because they were a people of mixed race. This information should help us to understand that there are no prerequisites for being the helper. You don't have to have position or popularity. You don't have to be an expert or extremely wealthy. Anybody can help somebody!

The other two men not only kept going, but they walked on the other side of the street. Why did they keep going? Was it that they were too consumed with their own agendas? Did they say to themselves, *"If he is still here when I come back, I will do something?"* And why did they cross over the other side of the street? Was the sight of the wounds too much for them? Did they not want to get blood on their shoes?

Why did the *Samaritan* stop? Maybe as the *Samaritan* approached this wounded, destitute man, he realized that it could have been him lying there! He had arrived moments earlier and been the one beaten, robbed and left for dead! Or, maybe he realized the man who he saw *half dead*, was still *half alive.* There was still half of a chance, half of an opportunity, half of a hope to reach his destination. Maybe, if given a helping hand, he could make it! He could get him back on his feet and he would succeed. *Sisterfriend,* maybe he knew what it was like to need a helping hand. If we would tell the truth, we do too!

The reality is none of us are where we are today, solely on our own merit. Somebody else had a hand in our development. As for me, it was the hand of my mother who gave up her own dreams of becoming a nurse to work three jobs to take care of her five children. It was the hand of my 10th grade teacher, Mrs. Washington, who spent her lunch hour everyday helping me fill out college applications. It has been the hand of my devoted husband who has been on the sidelines cheering me on, helping with the cooking and the cleaning, so that I could go back to school and further my education. *Sisterfriend*, whose hand was there for you? Who is your hand there for?

Daddy

Death was nothing new to me. My husband and I have stood by many bedsides and held the hands of someone as they breathed their last breath. But as someone told me, *it's different when it's your own.*

The doctor was calling with questions that I have never given a second thought. May we have permission to put in a feeding tube? Do you want us to remove the feeding tube? Do you want us to try surgery even though we don't think it will work? Do you want us to resuscitate?

How could I answer these questions for another individual, especially my *Daddy*? All I could think about was *Lord, could you please slow this experience down.*

I never thought about having to make decisions for my parents, they had always made decisions for me. I never imagined that my first decision concerning one of them would be a matter of life and death. I never dreamed that my first opportunity to pick out his clothes, would be the last outfit he would ever wear. Now those statements I made as a teenager like, *I want to make my own decisions* and *I know what I am doing* sounded foolish. I didn't want to make these decisions and I definitely did not know what I was doing. I remember looking over at my children with tears in their eyes as they were experiencing their first funeral. How could I soothe them—it was a first for me, the death of a parent!

In one week, seven days later, it was over. I had

made the most serious decisions of my life, had done the hardest things I had ever had to do, felt the deepest pain I had ever experienced, and it was over. My *Daddy* was dead and buried. I felt like I had aged 20 years!

Like I always do, I reflected on this experience to discover what I gained from it. And here is what I got...I learned that there is a time to be born and a time to die, and the time to die is just as important as the time to be born. I saw that we brought nothing into this world, and we truly will take nothing away. I experienced the true feeling of a clear conscious, when you know that you did the best you could. I learned that it is better to be left with memories of love and laughter, than of anger and bitterness (I'm glad I resolved my issues with my *Daddy* early on). But most of all I discovered another dimension of God's love. I found out that His strength is perfected in our weakness. *I will always love you Daddy!*

Heart

Much is said about the power of the tongue and how we should bridle this unruly evil. But before we can conquer what is coming out of our mouths, we must find its source. Where is the fountain that springs forth such negativity, skepticism, and criticism? What makes us say what we say? I believe that it is what is in our *hearts*!

A good man brings good things out of the good stored up in his heart, and an evil man brings evil things out of the evil stored up in his heart. For the mouth speaks what the heart is full of (Luke 6:45).

What is in your *hearts*? Is it full of envy, jealousy or possibly hatred? Maybe it is clouded with unforgiveness, hurt, and despair. Could it be tainted with self-righteousness, pride and haughtiness?

Maybe we should stop asking God for help with our tongues and allow Him to work on our *hearts*. The Psalmist says, *"Create in me a clean heart, O God; and renew a right spirit within me"* (Psalm 51:10).

God can take our hearts of stone and give us *hearts* of flesh. He can give us love and compassion that we never thought would be possible. He can give us the ability to look beyond one's faults and see their needs.

Sisterfriend, God is willing to do a *heart transplant* for anyone who will admit that they need a new *heart*. Admittance into His hospital only requires submission of our will for His will. Faith the size of a grain of mustard seed is enough anesthesia to allow you to make it through the surgery.

Don't delay! He has already found a donor just for you. His name is Jesus Christ.

Lord

Even as Sara obeyed Abraham, calling him lord; whose daughter ye are as long as ye do well, and are not afraid with any amazement (1 Peter 3:6).

I wonder how many daughters of Sara exists today? Sara spoke highly of Abraham to the extent that she called him *lord.* Now of course, we know that Abraham was not perfect, and so did Sara. But she was focused on his good points. She maintained her respect for him. The Bible teaches that we are to be daughters of Sara, meaning that we should do likewise.

*Sisterfriend, m*ost of us tend to accentuate the negatives in our husbands. We often highlight his faults and failures. We become very passionate about issues that need straightening out. We can well articulate our opinion and skillfully debate our issue in an argument! The tragedy is however; we are quite passive about opportunities to give praise. We are less verbal when a compliment is warranted.

Sisterfriend, I want my husband to hear me call him *lord.* In my voice, there is an encouraging word for his troubles, faith for his challenges, praise for his successes, and hope for his dreams. Some wise person once said, *"behind every successful man, there is a great woman."* Hopefully, it is his wife!

I know by now, most of you are saying, *So, do I just ignore his faults?* The answer is, *no.* I am saying you *cover* them in love. I am saying that you *speak* the truth in love. Ask God to season your speech with grace and teach you discretion. Your words should be *timely* and *helpful*! And ask for the Holy Spirit to help him have a heart to receive what you will say.

Finally, though you call him, *lord,* he is not God! The reality is your husband is not perfect, so it helps if you build up a cushion of *praise* for him. It will soften the blow when you have to speak to his less than *lord* behavior!

We Are Still Here!

We made it, *Sisterfriends!* In spite of the circumstances, through the storm and rain, we endured. *We are still here!* Do you realize how much inner strength we possess? We could have given up. We could have allowed life to cause us to surrender our hope. But when times get rough, you and I expose the "*W*" for woman, on our chest and accepted life's challenges. We made meals stretch and ends meet. We comforted others, while sick ourselves. We cared for our children, sometimes being both mother and father. We motivated our husbands and ministered to our friends. We were loyal to our jobs and devoted to our God. Who but a woman of faith could do all that and maintain her sanity?

Sure, you've made some mistakes – who hasn't? And maybe you didn't reach a few goals – who doesn't? The silver lining in the cloud is that if you live to see tomorrow, you will have another opportunity to try again.

So, let me be the first to congratulate you for a job well done. If no one else appreciates what you have done, I do. It encourages me to know that *Sisterfriends* like you still exist. By the way, *Sisterfriend,* God is proud of you also! And you know when He says *well done* blessings are on the way!

Moments of Meditation

Delight thyself also in the Lord; and he shall give thee the desires of thine heart. *Psalms 37:4*

God is our refuge and strength and a very present help in trouble. *Psalms 46:1*

For I know the thoughts that I think toward you, says the Lord, thoughts of peace, and not of evil, to give you an expected end. *Jeremiah 29:11*

Ask and it shall be given; seek and ye shall find knock and it shall be opened unto you: For everyone that asks receives; for he that seeks finds, and to him that knocks it shall be opened. *Matthew 7:7-8*

And let us not be weary in well doing; for in due season we shall reap if we faint not. *Galatians 6:9*

Let us hold fast the profession of our faith without wavering; for He is faithful that promised. Hebrews 10:23

But my God shall supply all your needs according to his riches in glory by Christ Jesus. *Philippians 4:19*

With men this is impossible; but with God all things are possible. *Matthew19:26*

When thou passest through the waters, I will be with thee; and through the rivers, they shall not overflow thee; When thou walkest through the fire thou shalt not be burned neither shall the flame kindle upon thee. *Isaiah 43:2*

Prayer Petition

Be careful for nothing; but in everything by prayer and supplication with thanksgiving let your request be made know unto God. Philippians 4:6

25 Ways to Be Good to Yourself

"... in thy presence is fullness of joy, at thy right hand there are pleasures forevermore:" Psalm 16:11

1. Exercise
2. Take a bubble bath
3. Read a book
4. Take a day off work (without being sick)
5. Call an old friend
6. Get a massage
7. Buy new makeup and undergarments
8. Rent your favorite movie
9. Give yourself a gift
10. Get a manicure/pedicure
11. Dress up/down for no special reason
12. Try a new hobby
13. Listen to your favorite music
14. Get help with chores around the house
15. Get organized
16. Learn to say no, and not feel guilty
17. Make a new friend
18. Keep a journal
19. Say affirmations every morning
20. Reevaluate your goals
21. Compliment yourself
22. Do something you've never done before
23. Be spontaneous
24. Reserve a daily devotional time
25. Accept love from others

www.ingramcontent.com/pod-product-compliance
Lightning Source LLC
LaVergne TN
LVHW051511070426
835507LV00022B/3049